Standards for the Board

SECOND EDITION

Edited by Tony Renton

First published March 1999
ISBN 0-7494-3081-8

© Crown Copyright 1999

Produced with funding from the Department for Education and Employment. Published by consent of the Secretary of State, Department for Education and Employment, and with the permission of the Controller of HMSO.

Published by the
Institute of Directors
116 Pall Mall
London SW1Y 5ED

Kogan Page
120 Pentonville Road
London N1 9JN

I warmly welcome the work that the Institute of Directors does to inform and educate directors about good business practice. I also support the continuing work of the IoD on improving the professionalism of directors in both the public and private sectors, and their encouragement and dissemination of good practice to their members and to the wider business community.

The Rt Hon Stephen Byers MP
SECRETARY OF STATE
FOR TRADE AND INDUSTRY

The first edition of the IoD's publication *Good Practice for Directors – Standards for the Board* (Institute of Directors, March 1995) was developed by the IoD in association with Henley Management College, with funding from the Employment Department (now DfEE). The original project was based upon extensive research and consultation. It employed a number of research methods: detailed literature reviews, questionnaires to both directors and expert opinion holders, focus groups, and one-to-one interviews with practising directors. The draft conclusions were then field-tested. The original *Standards* thus reflected the views and practice of hundreds of company directors and many boards in the UK.

However it was felt that developments in the field of corporate governance during recent years have been sufficient to justify a fresh look at good boardroom practice, resulting in the present substantially revised edition of these *Standards*. This revised edition has also benefited from DfEE support.

The project on which this publication is based was carried out under the guidance of a Steering Group set up by the Institute of Directors (IoD) and the Department for Education and Employment (DfEE).

In undertaking the process of revision, a research survey, focus groups of experienced directors and input from academics were again employed. These *Standards*, therefore, represent a collective view of good practice drawn from a very broad cross-section of companies in diverse settings. They cover both small and large firms, listed and private companies, companies in the public sector, and subsidiaries of both UK and foreign-owned companies.

Many of the changes from the first edition reflect no more than a change of perspective, or a different way of ordering the material. However, there are a number of significant changes, in part the result of a second look at some of the issues raised and in part the result of changes in what is perceived as good practice during the intervening years. More emphasis has been placed upon the relationship between a company and its board of directors, on the one hand, and the various parties or stakeholders associated with a company, on the other hand. The previous appendix on the legal duties and liabilities of company directors has been substantially revised and incorporated as a separate Part in the text. There is a new appendix summarising the Combined Code on Corporate Governance (June 1998). There is a much expanded Part discussing key areas of directors' knowledge and skills.

The aim throughout has been to provide a guide to good practice which is concise, readable and accurate. The layout has been simplified.

These *Standards* are the result of extensive consultation. I wish particularly to acknowledge the comments and constructive criticism offered by the members of the project Steering Group: John Carrington, Graham Cheetham, Richard Everard, and Nelson Hawkes. My colleagues Mark Watson and John Harper, lately Professional Development Director at the IoD, were responsible for much of the focus group facilitation; John Harper also helped greatly with the writing. Sherry Keys and Vanessa Crichton cheerfully and efficiently undertook a laborious secretarial and administrative task.

Tony Renton
London
March 1999

Standards for the Board

INTRODUCTION

The parties associated with a company

A company, in a free market economy, is an economic and social organisation transforming inputs into outputs and exchanging these in the market place. It is therefore at the centre of a complex web of socio-economic relationships. Whilst many of these relationships are circumscribed by law and regulation, the key factors in these relationships are not always obvious, since often many qualitative and non-quantifiable factors need to be considered. The board of directors, as custodian of the company's prosperity, must recognise and evaluate these qualitative factors in much of its decision-making.

The legal status of a company requires that two groups of interests warrant special treatment. These two groups are shareholders and creditors. The relationship of shareholders to a company is different from that of other associated parties in that it is based on property rights. For example, an equity share can be bought, sold or transferred, and entitles the investor to participate in the residual profits of the company, with liability limited to the amount of the investment. Shareholders also have a right to information about the company and can play a part in the formal decision-making of the company, primarily by participation in general shareholder meetings and by voting. Most importantly, shareholder interests are specifically protected by company law.

Creditors, whose normal legal right to be paid out of the assets of a company proprietor is diminished by shareholders' limited liability, are also given special legal protection. The position of boards and directors with respect to these two groups is dealt with in Part One below.

A company, however, has associated with it a number of other interests or parties, sometimes called "stakeholders", and its relations with such groups, for example, employees, customers and suppliers, are generally not affected by its corporate status. Obligations of a company to stakeholders – though not the mechanisms for enforcing a company's compliance with these obligations, the burden of which tends to bear heavily on directors personally – are virtually the same for any individual or organisation. (The position of employees is a little different, since the Companies Act 1985 imposes a fiduciary duty on directors to have regard in the performance of their functions to the interests of the company's employees in general). Nonetheless, to be successful, a board of directors must adopt policies for the company's dealings with stakeholders which take account of at least the commercial aspects of the company's relationship with them, and in addition there are often specific pieces of legislation which circumscribe a board's freedom of action in these dealings.

For example, boards will very often pay greater attention to their customers' needs and concerns than is strictly required by the laws designed to protect consumer interests. After all, it is mainly customers who generate income; all other parties associated with a company generate costs. Similarly, boards will often come to the view that it is unhelpful to deal with employees simply on the basis of a contractual buyer/seller relationship and will go beyond the rights and duties contained in present employment legislation and company law.

There is a large number of other parties who from time to time may take an interest in, and be in a position to influence, the company's goals and operations. Even where stakeholder interests are not protected by law, it is the job of the board of directors, as stewards of the company's survival and prosperity, to take a view as to how the company should relate to these stakeholders, and what extra-legal commitments it should make – from holding itself accountable at one extreme, through active co-operation, consideration and explanation, to ignoring at the other extreme.

On the one hand, some boards of directors take the view – sometimes explicitly stated as necessary in the company's own long-term interest – that their companies should act and be seen to act as "good corporate citizens", and attempt to be a positive force for good in such areas as protection of the environment, education, urban renewal, health, racial equality, and other areas of social concern. On the other hand, some boards take a position much closer to the strict limits prescribed by law and regulation.

Whatever standpoint in relation to stakeholders is adopted by the board is, of course, not immutable and no doubt will change as circumstances change. The important point is that the board recognises it has to take a view and maintain what it regards as a proper balance of interests.

In considering these matters and arriving at a balanced view, the board should always endeavour to meet its key purpose, which is **to ensure the company's prosperity by collectively directing the company's affairs, whilst meeting the appropriate interests of its shareholders and relevant stakeholders.**

It is for the board to judge, on a case-by-case basis, which stakeholders it treats as relevant and which of their interests it is appropriate to meet, taking into account the law and relevant regulations and the board's judgement of the commercial interests of the company.

The board's complex role

In pursuing its key purpose, a board of directors faces a uniquely demanding set of responsibilities and challenges, the complexity of which can be seen in some of the seemingly contradictory pressures it faces:

- *The board must simultaneously be entrepreneurial and drive the business forward while keeping it under prudent control.*

- *The board is required to be sufficiently knowledgeable about the workings of the company to be answerable for its actions, yet to be able to stand back from the day-to-day management of the company and retain an objective, long-term view.*

- *The board must be sensitive to the pressures of short-term issues and yet be informed about broader, long-term trends.*

- *The board must be knowledgeable about "local" issues and yet be aware of potential or actual non-local, increasingly international, competitive and other influences.*

- *The board is expected to be focused upon the commercial needs of its business while acting responsibly towards its employees, business partners and society as a whole.*

What are the Standards for?

It is implicit that within a company the board of directors is the principal agent of risk taking, enterprise, commercial and other judgement. However, there are particular ways of working as a board, particular tasks for the board to fulfil, and particular areas of knowledge and personal attributes with which directors would find it helpful to be equipped in order for the board to succeed in fulfilling its purpose. These matters are addressed in these *Standards*.

These *Standards* aim to:

- *provide guidelines of good practice, including statutory requirements, for company directors, which should inform the way in which they collectively and individually conduct board business and discharge their responsibilities;*

- *provide a framework within which company boards can develop, maintain and review their corporate governance policies and practices;*

- *help boards improve their own performance and, through this, the success of their companies. Sensible application of the* Standards *in individual companies will clarify the board's tasks and the way it conducts its affairs. The* Standards *can be used as a tool for re-appraising what the board does and how it does it, and for taking actions which might otherwise not have been taken. The* Standards *also highlight the attributes required of individual directors if a board is to operate successfully. Their use can also assist in the selection, induction, training and development of directors.*

The *Standards* complement both the substantial legal framework that has built up over many years and within which directors must carry out their duties – the legal duties and liabilities of directors are well documented in the IoD's publication *Guidelines for Directors* and are briefly summarised in Part One of this document – and the substantial body of existing material giving guidance about good practice in board procedures. They also complement the thinking about the working of the board and the accountability of directors expounded in various reports on corporate governance, culminating in the *Committee on Corporate Governance: The Combined Code* (The London Stock Exchange Ltd., 1998), which is summarised in the Appendix, pages 79-86 (the "Combined Code").

The *Standards* are applicable to commercial companies of all types and sizes. Moreover, with sensible adaptation, they will be applicable in other types of organisation, too.

Who are the Standards for?

The board is a working group of people collectively responsible for the company. Accordingly, these *Standards* are of prime value to the board as a whole since they focus principally upon what the board should address in order to conduct its affairs properly and effectively.

However, individual directors may wish to consider their own contribution to the board's performance and their own capabilities in the light of these *Standards*. Chairmen, in particular, may find them helpful as a basis for board appraisal and in ensuring that the board operates effectively.

How should the Standards be used?

These *Standards* should be used as a reference document, not a list of mandatory instructions. The benefits will accrue from the process of using them. There are no universal or single definitive answers to many of the issues raised.

The wide-ranging nature of the *Standards* means that each board can tailor them to its own circumstances. Interpretation will depend upon the size and type of the company as well as the circumstances it faces. The relevance and importance of the individual *Standards* to a particular board will be decided by that board.

The process of company direction is complex and partly intuitive; the *Standards* are intended to help the board maintain a firm and clear structure and good practice in its activities. The *Standards* are presented in four Parts, three of which can be used as checklists on their own. The board can refer to these checklists to identify gaps in its expertise, performance and ways of working which might then be addressed, whether through training and development, a change in the board's approach, and replacement of a director or adding to the board's number. For example:

- *The* Standards *can be used to help the board check that it is keeping its focus on strategy – particularly by using the checklists in Part Three (A1, B1-B5 and C1);*

- *The board can use Part Two (especially section 4) to review the efficiency and effectiveness with which it conducts its business;*

- *Part Two, section 2, and Part Three (C) can be used to review and support the development of the company's management, and to keep a clear distinction between the role of the board and that of the company management;*

- *Part One in particular will help the board review its compliance with legal requirements, the IoD's standards of corporate governance and of the Combined Code;*

- *Part Three (D) will help the board review its relationships with shareholders and with relevant parties with an interest in the company's affairs;*

- *Part Two, sections 1 and 4, and Part Four will help chairmen especially to plan the development of the board.*

Index of some applications of the Standard

(Page numbers are shown against each Aspect and Action)	DEFINING & IDENTIFYING	DECIDING	IMPROVING	ASSESSING
ASPECTS OF DIRECTION	**ACTION**			
1 The board's role, powers and responsibilities	30	34		4-5
2 The board's tasks	42-61		42-61	42-61
3 Board composition/structure	64-66, 83	32-33		
4 Board meetings and organisation	37-38, 81		37-38	
5 Board effectiveness	27-39	23,28	39	39
6 Delineation between board and management	34-36, 54-57	34-36		
7 Director selection	64-66	32-33		
8 Director development and training		25		
9 Directors' fiduciary duties	14-19			
10 Directors' attributes	64-71			
11 Directors' knowledge	72-78			
12 Delegation to management	54-57		54-57	54-57
13 Board accountability	58-61		58-61	58-61
14 Company vision, mission and values	46-49		46-49	46-49
15 Directing strategy and structure	50-53		50-53	50-53
16 Responsibility to shareholders and relevant stakeholders	58-61, 84	2-4, 23-24	58-61	58-61
17 Company performance				48-49
18 Role of the chairman	82	28-39		
19 Role of the non-executive director	81, 83, 86			

Glossary of key terms

A number of terms are used in the text. To avoid confusion, definitions are given here.

VISION A view of a desired future state for the company which the company will ideally attain.

MISSION A statement of what needs to be done in order to achieve the envisioned state, preferably quantified.

GOALS Measurable targets which relate to the achievement of the mission.

VALUES A set of principles and standards of conduct which inform the company's affairs.

STRATEGY A statement of the business the company will undertake, how it will carry out its business, and the resources it will deploy, in order to fulfil its mission.

OBJECTIVES Measurable targets which relate to the achievement of a strategy.

POLICIES Statements relating to the activities of the company and the way in which they should be carried out.

DETERMINE This covers a spectrum of possible action from "creating" at one extreme through "participative scrutiny and testing with management" to "ratifying" at the other.

STAKEHOLDERS Individuals or groups, apart from shareholders, whom the board judges on occasion to have an appropriate interest in, and/or influence over, the company's operations and the achievement of the company's goals. Such groups are likely to include, apart from creditors who have special legal protection, *inter alia*, employees, suppliers, customers, competitors, regulators, local communities, analysts, banks, lobbyists, pressure groups, media, trade associations, European, national and local governments, and stock exchanges (where appropriate).

CHAIRMAN The person (of either sex) who leads the board and manages its business.

MANAGING DIRECTOR The director who is empowered by the board to manage the company day-to-day, lead the employees, and ensure that the board's decisions are properly and effectively implemented. Sometimes called chief executive.

NON-EXECUTIVE DIRECTOR A director who, broadly, does not take part in the day-to-day operations of the company, confines his or her role to that of preparing for and attending board meetings, and is not an employee of the company.

Standards for the Board

PART ONE:
The Legal Duties and
Liabilities of Company Directors
and Good Practice

This summary is for guidance only and refers to the duties and liabilities of company directors. It reflects the law of England and Wales as at March 1st 1999 relating to directors of a company incorporated under the Companies Act 1985 (the "Act"), various provisions of the Insolvency Act 1986, and also what is good practice in corporate governance. Company directors should seek advice from their legal advisers if they are unclear about their current or potential legal position.

Useful reference text books dealing with the legal duties and liabilities of directors are: Gore-Browne on *Companies*, Tolley's *Company Law*, and *Company Directors: Law and Liability* edited by Sinclair, Vogel and Snowden.

General

- A director is a person empowered under a company's Articles of Association to direct, and to share responsibility with the other directors for, the governance of its affairs. Directors are appointed in accordance with the Articles of the company, but it is possible, in law, for a person who has not been appointed or has been appointed improperly to assume the role of director (a "shadow" director) and in so doing to become subject to many of the legal duties and obligations which apply to any director. This can also happen when a person engaged as an adviser is admitted to the decision-making process of a board. While a person is not deemed a shadow director by reason only that the directors act on advice given by him or her in a professional capacity, if an adviser participates in making board decisions he or she may be deemed to be acting as a shadow director, and will be liable under some of the legal duties and obligations which apply to any director. For this reason, the formal status of people attending board meetings should be made clear by the chairman, when those other than board members are present.

- There is no single comprehensive legal code of conduct for directors. Their duties and liabilities arise under common law, the Act, and a variety of other statutes, regulations and rules.

- Directors' duties are owed to the company only. In addition, directors must have regard to the interests of the company's shareholders, employees, the general public under certain environmental, health and safety legislation, and (if the company is or may be insolvent) creditors.

- All directors on the board share their legal responsibilities equally, whether they are executive or non-executive directors, and regardless of any particular duties under service agreements as employees.

- In general, directors are not liable for the company's debts or losses, unless they have given personal guarantees; but they may be made personally liable if they have acted in breach of their duties.

- For the purposes of wrongful trading, a director is judged by a legally defined standard. Failure to meet the standard may result in personal liability.

Constitutional powers

- Directors must not exceed the objects of the company under its Memorandum of Association, and must also operate within any limitations on their powers that may be imposed by its Articles.

Care and diligence

- Directors must carry out their functions with reasonable skill, care and diligence and may be liable if they are negligent. A higher standard of care is required of a director who has particular skills or professional qualifications in relation to matters where those skills or qualifications have particular relevance.

- Directors should try to attend all board meetings, being absent only with good reason. Persistent non-attendance may amount to a breach of duty. Under the Articles of some companies the director may lose office if no board meetings are attended during a stated period.

Probity

Directors owe fiduciary duties to the company, which means that they are required to act in good faith in the best interests of the company; exercise their powers for the proper purposes for which they were conferred, and not place themselves in a position where there is a conflict (actual or potential) between their duties to the company and their personal interests (or the interests of any associated organisation or person) or duties to third parties. Fiduciary obligations can apply in circumstances which are not always obvious, and where no intentional dishonesty is involved.

The implications of this arise in various ways. For example:

1 Boards should comply with relevant laws, regulations and codes of practice, refrain from anti-competitive practices, and honour obligations and commitments. Individual directors must at all times comply with the law and should endeavour to ensure that their company at all times complies with the law governing its operations.

2 Although not a legal obligation, each director should at all times respect the truth and act honestly in business dealings and in the exercise of all responsibilities as a director. It follows, for example, that a director should not obtain, attempt to obtain, or accept, any bribe, secret commission or illegal inducement of any sort. Integrity should be the hallmark of each board

member's conduct in decision-making, uninfluenced by shareholdings, or by business, political or personal commitments and relationships external to his or her company duties.

3   The company's assets and resources must be applied only for proper purposes. The directors will be liable for the loss caused to the company and/or to restore the company's assets if they misapply them.

4   The directors must exercise their powers and apply company assets and resources in the interests of the company, not for any ulterior purpose or to benefit themselves or anyone else.

5   As a rule, a director cannot enter into an agreement with a third party under which he or she fetters his or her power to exercise an independent judgement except where he or she believes in good faith that it is in the interest of the company to do so.

6   A director must not take advantage of his or her position as a director to gain, directly or indirectly, a personal advantage or an advantage for any associated person unless permitted by the company's constitution or the situation has been disclosed to the company in general meeting and the company has consented.

   a   *A director must not make improper use of information acquired by virtue of his or her position as a director. This prohibition applies irrespective of whether or not the director or any associated person would gain directly or indirectly a personal advantage or whether or not the company might be harmed.*

   b   *Directors should not use inside information for gain and will be liable to account to the company for their gain (i.e. profit not authorised by a shareholder resolution or in accordance with the company's Articles) if they use their position to make a secret profit.*

c   *A director should make sure that any information which is not in the public domain and which would have a significant effect on the company's share price if publicly available is not provided to anyone who may be influenced to subscribe for, buy or sell shares, or may advise others to do so. Such information includes, but is not limited to: profit forecasts, proposed share issues, borrowings, impending take-overs, impending litigation, significant changes in operations, new products, new discoveries, and financial problems. Listing Rules require directors of a company listed on the Stock Exchange to make adequate and timely disclosure to the Stock Exchange.*

d   *A director must not buy or sell shares while in possession of confidential information as a director of a company which, if disclosed publicly, would be likely materially to affect the price of the company's shares. It is good practice for the board to lay down precisely when shares can be traded by a director of the company, subject to legal or regulatory restrictions. Companies listed on the Stock Exchange must require their directors to comply with a code of dealing which is no less exacting than the Model Code of the Stock Exchange.*

e   *Good practice requires the board to develop guidelines on the circumstances in which benefits to be received by a director or an associated person are of sufficient magnitude that the approval of the shareholders should be sought, even if not required by law. The board should inform shareholders of these guidelines. A director of a company listed on the Stock Exchange must observe those Listing Rules relating to any benefits that a director or an associated person may receive from the company by way of an issue of shares or any other transaction of a similar nature.*

7   A company director has a general duty to avoid any actual or potential conflict between his or her own personal interests,

or the interests of any associated organisation or person, and his or her duties to the company.

Under the Act, if a director, a member of his/her immediate family or other connected person (as defined by the Act), has a personal interest in some transaction involving the company, the director must declare that interest to the board.

Directors must disclose to the company their interests (including the interests of their spouse and dependent children and certain trusts or companies controlled by such persons) in shares or debentures of the company (and group companies). The company is required to maintain a register, open to inspection, of these interests.

Depending on the company's Articles, the director may be excluded from participating in a decision about or voting on a particular matter and/or from being counted in the quorum for the board meeting at which it is considered.

In the extreme case of continuing material conflict of interest good practice requires the director to resign from the board.

Some examples where disclosure of interest would be appropriate are:

a   *when a firm bids for a contract with the company, and a board member, or an associated party, has a financial interest in the firm or is a director of it;*

b   *when a relative of a board member is on the staff or the board of an important supplier or customer;*

c   *when a board member is party to information which is of commercial value to their own, or an associated party's, business or organisation;*

d *when a director is appointed to a board at the instigation of a third party with a substantial interest in the company, such as a major shareholder or a creditor. The director's duty is to make a contribution in the interests of the company and not in the particular interest of the sponsor. If obligations to a third party preclude a director from taking an independent position on an issue, it is good practice to disclose the situation to the rest of the company board and it is for the board to judge whether or not the individual director should take part in the board's consideration of the particular issue.*

In the examples above, or similar circumstances, confidential matters should not be disclosed to the interested parties without the prior agreement of the company board.

8 In general terms, members of a board should accept collective responsibility for the decisions of the board as loyal members of the board. This does not mean that a director should not be prepared, if necessary, to express disagreement with colleagues, including the chairman or managing director, but it does mean that he or she should accept that resignation or dismissal may sometimes be the ultimate consequence of sustained protest on a matter of company policy, conscience or principle.

When a director concludes that he or she is unable to acquiesce in a decision of the board, some or all of the following steps should be considered:

a *making his/her dissent and its possible consequences clear to the board as a means of seeking to influence the decision;*

b *asking for additional legal, accounting or other professional advice (the Combined Code) recommends that the company should meet the expenses incurred);*

c	*asking that the decision be postponed to the next meeting to allow time for further consideration and informal discussion;*

d	*tabling a statement of dissent or writing to the chairman and asking that the statement or letter be minuted;*

e	*calling a special board meeting to consider the matter;*

f	*resigning and considering advising the appropriate regulator.*

A director who chooses to resign on a point of principle or other important matter should disclose the reasons for resignation to shareholders or to the appropriate regulator, though a director should bear in mind the duty not to disclose confidential information.

Transactions within the company

The Act imposes detailed restrictions on certain types of transaction between a company and any of its directors, their families, or other connected persons (as defined in the Act).

- Loans by a company to a director of more than £5,000 are prohibited, subject to certain detailed exceptions. Nor is the company allowed to provide a guarantee or other security for any loans to a director from another source. Any transaction entered into in contravention of these restrictions is voidable at the instance of the company and any director who authorises the transaction is liable to account to the company for any gain that he or she has made by the transaction and to indemnify the company for any loss or damage resulting from the transaction. A director who authorised a company to enter into a transaction knowing or having reasonable cause to believe that the company was contravening these provisions is guilty of a criminal offence.

- Complex provisions of the Act deal with other types of credit transaction, which may be permitted in certain circumstances.

- A transfer of non-cash assets between a director, his family or other connected persons (as defined in the Act) and the company, where the value exceeds specified limits, is only permitted with the approval by resolution of the shareholders in general meeting, subject to detailed exceptions. If shareholder approval is not given, the transaction is voidable at the instance of the company and any director who authorised the transaction is liable to account to the company for any gain that he/she has made by the transaction and to indemnify the company for any loss or damage resulting from the transaction.

- Directors' service agreements under which the directors' employment may continue for a period of more than five years (during which period it cannot be terminated by the company by notice or can only be so terminated in specified circumstances) must be approved by resolution of the shareholders in general meeting. It is recommended here that service agreements are terminable on one year's notice.

Administration

- Directors are responsible for the company's due administration, including maintenance of proper accounting records, minutes of meetings, and filing information at Companies House. In practice the directors can delegate these duties and the company secretary may handle much of the administration, but this does not relieve the directors of the ultimate responsibility.

- There are numerous statutory provisions covering such topics as employee relations, health and safety, consumer protection, environmental protection, data protection and taxation. Some of these create offences of personal liability under which directors may face penalties if the company fails to comply with the statutory requirements.

- Directors are also subject to specific duties and restrictions under the Financial Services Act 1986, particularly in relation to the company's shares, in the case of a company limited by shares, and debentures.

Preparation of accounts

- Under the Act, the directors must ensure that proper accounting records are kept by the company, they must prepare and approve the annual report and accounts which comply with the Act, they must lay the accounts and report before the shareholders in general meeting and they must ensure that the company sends copies to all its shareholders and to the Registrar of Companies. The period allowed for laying and delivering report and accounts is generally ten months after the end of the relevant accounting reference period for a private company and seven months after the end of that period for a public company (with a three month extension in each case for an overseas company).

- Small and medium-sized companies are exempt from certain requirements relating to the preparation of accounts. In addition, a private company may by resolution elect to dispense with the laying of accounts and report before the shareholders in general meeting. Such exemptions often apply in subsidiary companies.

Insolvency

If a company becomes or is about to become insolvent, the Insolvency Act 1986 imposes various duties and responsibilities on the directors, which are designed to protect the interests of the company's creditors. In particular:

- The directors may be liable for wrongful trading unless they take all proper steps to minimise the creditors' potential losses, once they knew or **ought to have concluded** that there was no reasonable prospect that insolvent liquidation could be avoided.

- Breach of this provision of the Insolvency Act 1986 may result in the directors being ordered by a court to contribute to the assets of the company, and/or disqualification.

Disqualification

- A director can be disqualified, under the Company Directors Disqualification Act 1986, from being a director or from otherwise being involved in the management of a company for any period between two and fifteen years in addition to incurring civil and criminal liabilities. A court must disqualify a director of a company which has at any time become insolvent where that person's conduct as a director makes him or her, in the court's opinion, unfit to be concerned in the "management" (including direction) of a company. A court may also disqualify a director who has been guilty of serious or persistent offences in connection with the direction and/or management of a company, or who has been guilty of wrongful trading, fraud or breach of duty.

- A shareholder, as well as others, may apply to the court for a disqualification order. If a disqualified person acts as a director or is involved in the management of a company, he or she may be imprisoned for up to two years or fined or both and will be personally liable for the debts of that company.

Effectiveness

- The board should exercise leadership, enterprise and judgement, combined with prudent control, in directing the company so as to achieve its continuing prosperity, and always attempt to act in the best interests of the company as a whole. The board is responsible for ensuring that the company is financially viable and properly managed so as to protect and enhance the interests of the company over time. Each director should endeavour to ensure that the board fulfils its key purpose of safeguarding and improving the company's prosperity.

- The chairman of the board should endeavour to make certain that the role of the board and the key tasks of the board are properly understood by all the board members.

- Directors have a statutory duty of care and diligence (see above, page 13).

Accountability

- The duties of the board are owed to the company, but, in evaluating the interests of the company, a board of directors is accountable to the shareholders as a whole for the stewardship of the company.

- In addition, various Acts of Parliament have imposed broader responsibilities on companies and directors so that directors must often evaluate their actions in a wide social context and must often be conscious of the impact of their business on society. Particular attention should be paid to the environment, questions of occupational health and safety, employee relations, equal opportunity for employees, the impact of comp rules and consumer protection rules, and other legislati regulatory initiatives that may arise from time to time

- Over and above any legal or regulatory constraints, in deciding what is in the best interest of the company and its continuing prosperity, the board may wish on occasion to take into account the interests of stakeholders – individuals and groups, apart from shareholders – where the board judges they have an appropriate interest in or influence over the achievement of company objectives and the way in which these objectives are achieved. In certain circumstances the board may judge that the company's intentions or actions should be explained or even justified to them. This is likely to be particularly the case at times of major change or crisis (for example, large redundancy programmes, environmental disasters, take-over bids).

Openness

- Although not a legal obligation, it is good practice for directors to be as open and honest with their boards as possible.

- The board is responsible for communicating fully with shareholders and aligning the company with the latters' interests. The board must ensure the company complies with its legal obligations as to the disclosure of information.

- There should be sufficient transparency about the activities of the board in particular, and the company in general, to secure the confidence and trust of employees, customers, suppliers and the community which the company serves, without sacrificing commercial confidentiality. Reasonable transparency is a pre-requisite for worthwhile relationships with all the parties associated with a company. This goes beyond the duty that directors owe to the company and beyond the discharge of their duties of disclosure created by the Act.

- However, the board must take care to protect such information as the company holds in confidence. This applies equally to commercially and personally confidential information affecting the company and its employees, customers, suppliers, business partners or others. In addition, the company must comply with the legislation on data protection.

- Similarly, a director must not disclose, or allow to be disclosed, confidential information received in the course of the exercise of his/her duties as a director, unless that disclosure has been authorised by the board of the company or is required by law. Trade secrets, matters that are an intellectual property right of the company, processes and methods, advertising and promotional programmes, and statistics affecting financial results, in particular, must not be disclosed.

- It is good practice for the board to ensure that there is a policy on openness and confidentiality of information which it regularly monitors and reviews. The board should also ensure that its own actions are consistent with this policy.

Director development

- Boards should try and ensure that all directors keep abreast of both practical and theoretical developments in company direction to ensure that their expertise is constantly relevant. Continuous and rapid change is the norm in business and it is the responsibility of a director continually and systematically to add to his or her knowledge, skill and expertise; it is not enough to match present good practice and thereafter regard oneself as adequately equipped for the future.

Standards
for the Board

PART TWO:
The Effective Board

The board of directors should be the principal agent of enterprise, risk-taking and commercial judgement within a company; the board should be the body that considers and decides those matters that will determine a company's prosperity. These matters are to do with the direction in which the company should be heading, how it will get there, how it performs and how it is perceived (see Part Three: Tasks of the Board and Indicators of Good Practice).

In all that it does the board should focus on its key purpose, namely, **to ensure the company's prosperity by collectively directing the company's affairs, whilst meeting the appropriate interests of its shareholders and relevant stakeholders.** This part of *Standards* addresses the essential matters that underlie a board's effectiveness in achieving this purpose.

A board may be composed of brilliant individuals and yet be ineffective. It can only fulfil its true potential as a board if it is properly selected, collectively organised and led. These activities are normally undertaken by the chairman of the board, part of whose role is to manage the board's business and act as its facilitator and guide. (Where the managing director is also the chairman, it is important that these two distinct roles are properly separated and that sufficient attention is given to carrying out the chairman's role effectively. The board should not be just an executive team).

The matters covered in this Part, therefore, can also be viewed as a list of key issues which a chairman should address, and make sure that the board addresses, in order to maximise the effectiveness of the board as a working group.

Many of the statements in this Part may appear to be self-evident; nonetheless, they are provided as a comprehensive checklist. A board should assess whether or not each of the actions described is appropriate to meet its specific circumstances, needs and current practice. An action plan can then be made.

The *Standards* in this Part cover:

1   *Devising board composition and organisation*

2   *Clarifying of board and management responsibilities*

3   *Planning and managing board and board committee meetings*

4   *Developing the effectiveness of the board*

"Executive" directors as such are not recognised in law. The term generally refers to individuals who have two roles – a board role and a senior management role. Although legally they are directors all of the time, the characteristics of their management role are different and additional to their director role. The management role lies outside the scope of this document; standards for senior managers are published in *Senior Management Standards: Second Edition* (The Management Charter Initiative, 1998).

Neither are the *Standards* in this Part concerned with the detail of board procedures. Publications by the Institute of Directors, the Institute of Chartered Secretaries and Administrators and others cover the substantial body of knowledge that already exists on board procedures.

The following short list of general board procedures adopted by a leading UK company is shown as an example of current good practice. Smaller companies may well find that less elaborate procedures suffice, and in particular may not delegate decision-making powers to committees of the board, but the example is nonetheless instructive.

EXAMPLE OF A STATEMENT OF GENERAL BOARD PROCEDURES: A MAJOR UK BANKING GROUP

1. Board meetings

- Board meetings will normally be held monthly on the second Tuesday of the month. There are no meetings in January or August.

- The quorum for a meeting is seven directors, with at least one director being an independent non-executive (as identified in the Group's Annual Report and Accounts).

2. Role of the board

The board is responsible for:

- guarding and serving the interests of shareholders and other stakeholders, including responsibilities to customers, investors, staff, suppliers and the community at large;

- determining the aims of the Group and agreeing the strategy, plans, policies and individual investment and divestment proposals for achieving those aims;

- monitoring the progress of the Group in implementing the strategy, plans and policies;

- ensuring the Group has appropriate leadership and vision;

- monitoring the performance of the Group's executive management and ensuring that management is of the right calibre;

- ensuring the Group is run with integrity, complies with all legal and regulatory requirements and statements of best practice and conducts its business in accordance with high ethical standards.

3. Composition of the board

- The board has the power to appoint additional directors to the board;

- The board shall be given notice at a prior board meeting of the intention to appoint any additional directors;

- Executive directors shall retire from the board on relinquishing their executive appointments, but shall be eligible for re-appointment for an initial term of three years;

- Directors retiring at age 70 in accordance with S293 (3) of the Companies Act shall not seek re-election unless invited by the board (on advice from the Nomination Committee) to do so;

- The board shall elect the chairman and deputy chairman annually at the March meeting and they shall hold office for one year from 1 May following their election.

4. Delegation of Powers

The board has delegated specific powers, as set out in the terms of reference to the following committees:

i   Chairman's Committee

ii   Group Audit and Compliance Committee (with power to sub-delegate to Business Audit and Compliance Committees)

iii   Capital Committee

iv   Nomination Committee

v   Remuneration Committee

vi   Directors' Share Dealing Committee

vii   Special Matters Committee

1. Board composition and organisation

1.1 Determine and regularly review board composition and identify any need for changes in board membership (including the chairman) and the timing thereof.

1.2 Determine and regularly review each individual's role and responsibilities and how these interrelate between directors.

1.3 Identify any gaps or (undesirable) overlap between individual directors' roles and responsibilities; plan and execute corrective action required.

1.4 Select, appoint, induct, develop or remove board members or company secretary.

1.5 Ensure regular and rigorous appraisal of the competence of all board members.

1.6 Identify and select external advisers when in-house expertise is insufficient.

ACTION LIST FOR DECIDING BOARD COMPOSITION

- Consider the ratio and number of executive and non-executive directors.

- Consider the energy, experience, knowledge, skills and personal attributes of current and prospective directors in relation to the future needs of the board as a whole, and develop specifications and processes for new appointments, as necessary.

- Consider the cohesion, dynamic tension and diversity of the board and its leadership by the chairman.

- Make and review succession plans for directors and the company secretary.

- Where necessary, remove incompetent or unsuitable directors or the company secretary, taking relevant legal, contractual, ethical, and commercial matters into account.

- Agree proper procedures for electing a chairman and appointing the managing director and other directors.

- Identify potential candidates for the board, make selection and agree terms of appointment and remuneration. New appointments should be agreed by every board member.

- Provide new board members with a comprehensive induction to board processes and policies, inclusion to the company and to their new role.

- Monitor and appraise each individual's performance, behaviour, knowledge, effectiveness and values rigorously and regularly.

- Identify development needs and training opportunities for existing and potential directors and the company secretary.

2. The powers, roles and responsibilities of the board and management respectively

2.1 Define the powers and roles the board reserves to itself. (See the example on page 35).

2.2 Review the relevance of the company's Memorandum and Articles of Association, pertinent legislation and other prescriptive guidelines.

2.3 Specify the powers and roles to be delegated to individual directors, including the chairman.

2.4 Specify the powers to be delegated to board committees and determine their terms of reference, life span, leadership and membership. (Examples of the most common board committees are on page 38).

2.5 Empower the managing director to implement the decisions of the board and other specific matters not reserved to the board itself. Confirm such empowerment by a formal resolution of the board.

EXAMPLE OF A STATEMENT OF RESERVED POWERS

The following example of a statement of the board's reserved powers is not exhaustive and, conversely, includes some matters that may not be relevant to a particular board, but it is indicative of the sorts of matters that the board should not delegate to management.

1. Statutory obligations

1.1 Approval of:

- the final dividend;
- the Annual Report and Accounts;
- circulars to shareholders, including those convening general meetings.

1.2 Consideration of:

- the interim dividend and Report;
- returns to overseas stock exchanges, if necessary.

1.3 Recommending to shareholders:

- changes to the Memorandum and Articles of Association;
- proposals relating to the appointment of auditors and approval of the audit fee.

2. Strategic and financial matters

2.1 Consideration of:

- the company's vision and mission;
- strategy;
- the company's progress against plans and budgets.

2.2 Approval of:

- Treasury, risk management and capital policies, including funding and the issue of ordinary shares, preference shares and loan capital;

- capital expenditure, acquisitions, joint ventures and disposals in excess of the discretionary power of the managing director;

- significant changes in accounting policy.

3. Personnel matters

3.1 Approval of:

- the appointment and removal of the managing director, other executive directors, and the company secretary;

- the appointment and removal of other directors on the recommendations of the Nomination Committee;

- the remuneration of directors where it is not set by the Remuneration Committee;

- the roles, duties and discretionary powers of the chairman and managing director;

- the arrangement of liability insurance for directors and officers.

4. Other matters

4.1 Approval of:

- any matter which would have a material effect on the company's financial position, liabilities, future strategy or reputation;

- contracts not in the ordinary course of the company's business;

- the company Code of Conduct, if it has one.

4.2 Delegation of:

- the board's powers and authority to committees of the board, such committees to be under an obligation to report back to the board.

3. Meetings of the board and its committees

3.1 Establish, maintain and develop reporting and meeting procedures for the board and its committees.

3.2 Determine policy for the frequency, purpose, conduct and duration of meetings and, especially, the setting of agenda. (Directors have the right to add items to agenda if they wish).

3.3 Create comprehensive agenda covering all the necessary and appropriate issues through the year, while also including important immediate issues.

3.4 Assign tasks and objectives to individual members including, especially, the chairman, managing director, finance director, and company secretary, and agree the working relationships between them.

3.5 Define and review regularly the information needs of the board.

3.6 Adopt efficient and timely methods for informing and briefing board members prior to meetings.

3.7 Maintain proper focus on the board's key role and tasks, ensuring that all the major strategic issues affecting the company's viability, reputation and prosperity are addressed.

3.8 Allow sufficient time for important matters to be discussed thoroughly.

3.9 Encourage all directors to attend all board meetings and to contribute appropriately to discussion, drawing on the full range of relevant opinions, knowledge, skills and experience.

3.10 Draw together the pertinent points from discussions in a timely way in order to reach well-informed decisions that command consensus.

3.11 Ensure that adequate minutes are kept and that board attendance and board decisions are properly recorded.

EXAMPLES OF BOARD COMMITTEES

Three committees of the board are recommended by the various codes of good governance and are required under the Stock Exchange Listing Rules. These are:

Audit committee

This committee is intended to provide a link between auditor and board independent of the company's executives, since the latter are responsible for the company's accounting rules and procedures that are the subject of the audit. The committee may thus help the board discharge its responsibility with regard to the validity of published financial statements. The Combined Code recommends that this committee should include at least three non-executive directors.

Remuneration committee

As a matter of good practice, executive directors should not be responsible for determining their own remuneration. The Combined Code on Corporate Governance recommends that this should be the remit of a remuneration committee made up wholly or mainly of non-executive directors.

Nomination committee

As a matter of good practice, the selection process of directors should be carried out by this committee, which then makes recommendations to the full board. Non-executive directors should form a majority of this committee.

Many small companies merge the remuneration and nomination committees.

4. The effectiveness of the board as a working group

4.1 Set and achieve objectives for continuous improvement in the quality and effectiveness of board performance, including performance in a crisis.

4.2 Review regularly the degree to which the board's objectives are achieved.

4.3 Review regularly the quality of the board's decisions, advice and information received and consequent actions taken.

4.4 Consider the impact on board effectiveness of directors' attitudes (to handling risk, failure, ethical issues, change, commitment and challenge), their interpersonal relationships and their decision-making styles.

4.5 Identify and influence the strengths and weaknesses of individual directors where these affect the performance of the board as a whole.

4.6 Take appropriate action(s) – including the use of training and external specialists – to maximise the efficiency and effectiveness of board work.

Standards
for the Board

PART THREE:
Tasks of the
Board and Indicators
of Good Practice

The key purpose of the board is to ensure the company's prosperity by collectively directing the company's affairs, whilst meeting the appropriate interests of its shareholders and relevant stakeholders. It is for the board to judge, on a case-by-case basis, which stakeholders it treats as "relevant" and which of their interests it is appropriate to meet, taking into account the law, relevant regulations and commercial considerations.

The board can be helped greatly in the achievement of this purpose by carrying out the relevant tasks described in this Part.

The *Standards* in this Part cover:

- *Establishing vision, mission and values*

- *Setting strategy and structure*

- *Delegating to management*

- *Exercising accountability to shareholders and being responsible to relevant stakeholders*

The board should decide which tasks it needs to carry out in order to achieve its overall purpose and identify which tasks it carries out at present. It can thus identify any gaps between what it does and what it needs to do.

The board will also be encouraged to focus on those tasks that it must – or wishes to – undertake itself and to decide which should more properly be carried out by senior management.

The indicators of good practice illustrate what actions are required to be taken for the successful completion of each of the tasks of the board. These indicators are intended to provide a comprehensive checklist for a board to assess whether it is addressing the tasks effectively and to decide what action, if any, is required.

However the indicators are not prescriptive or universal. Each board will need to consider those indicators which are appropriate and relevant to its own situation and circumstances. For example, small privately-owned companies would not be concerned with many issues which are peculiar to large listed companies. The indicators are numerous; they are defined so as to allow scope for interpretation.

AN OVERVIEW OF THE TASKS OF THE BOARD AND INDICATORS OF GOOD PRACTICE

A. Establish vision, mission and values

A.1 Determine the company's vision and mission to guide and set the pace for its current operations and future development.

A.2 Determine the values to be promoted throughout the company.

A.3 Determine and review company goals.

A.4 Determine company policies.

B. Set strategy and structure

B.1 Review and evaluate present and future opportunities, threats and risks in the external environment; and current and future strengths, weaknesses and risks relating to the company.

B.2 Determine strategic options, select those to be pursued, and decide the means to implement and support them.

B.3 Determine the business strategies and plans that underpin the corporate strategy.

B.4 Ensure that the company's organisational structure and capability are appropriate for implementing the chosen strategies.

C. Delegate to management

C.1 Delegate authority to management, and monitor and evaluate the implementation of policies, strategies and business plans.

C.2 Determine monitoring criteria to be used by the board.

C.3 Ensure that internal controls are effective.

C.4 Communicate with senior management.

D. Exercise accountability to shareholders and be responsible to relevant stakeholders

D.1 Ensure that communications both to and from shareholders and relevant stakeholders are effective.

D.2 Understand and take into account the interests of shareholders and relevant stakeholders.

D.3 Monitor relations with shareholders and relevant stakeholders by the gathering and evaluation of appropriate information.

D.4 Promote the goodwill and support of shareholders and relevant stakeholders.

A. Establish vision, mission and values

A.1 Determine the company's vision and mission to guide and set the pace for its current operations and future development

☐ *Does your board determine the vision and mission? If so, are the company's vision and mission...*

1.1 ☐ The result of a process led by either the chairman or managing director?

1.2 ☐ Contributed to and endorsed by all the board members?

1.3 ☐ Championed by the entire board throughout the company?

1.4 ☐ Influenced by the views of employees and known and understood by them?

1.5 ☐ Likely to promote the desired culture and ethos of the company?

1.6 ☐ Consistent with a level of risk-taking acceptable to the board?

1.7 ☐ Sure to stimulate and foster innovation?

1.8 ☐ Reviewed proactively at appropriate times?

1.9 ☐ Informed, when appropriate, by the views of shareholders and relevant stakeholders?

1.10 ☐ Sufficiently well founded to survive changes in board membership?

If so, is the company's vision...

1.11 ☐ Inspiring and challenging, yet realistic and practicable?

1.12 ☐ Consistent with the mission and values?

If so, is the company's mission...

1.13 ☐ Informed by external opinion and advice when necessary?

1.14 ☐ Consistent with the company's values and the requirements of the vision?

What action, if any, is required?...

A.2 Determine the values to be promoted throughout the company

☐ *Does your board determine the values?*
If so, are they...

2.1 ☐ Consistent with, and supportive of, the achievement of the vision and mission?

2.2 ☐ Explicit, unambiguous and feasible, to provide guidance and encouragement?

2.3 ☐ Championed by the board?

2.4 ☐ Influenced by the views of the employees?

2.5 ☐ Affected by the interests of shareholders and any relevant stakeholders?

2.6 ☐ Embedded in the company's culture?

2.7 ☐ Frequently reviewed for their efficacy?

What action, if any, is required?...

A. Establish vision, mission and values

A.3 Determine and review company goals

☐ *Does your board determine the company goals?*
If so, are they...

3.1 ☐ Consistent with the company's mission?

3.2 ☐ Clearly stated?

3.3 ☐ Realistic and achievable?

3.4 ☐ Measurable?

3.5 ☐ Agreed by the board?

3.6 ☐ Supported by individual directors?

What action, if any, is required?...

A.4 Determine company policies

☐ *Does your board determine the company's policies?*
If so, are they...

4.1 ☐ Actively promoted by the board?

4.2 ☐ Sufficiently resourced to be effective?

4.3 ☐ Consistent with company values?

4.4 ☐ Specifically influenced by the contributions of employees?

4.5 ☐ Unambiguous statements, indicating desired behaviour?

4.6 ☐ Informed by the appropriate views of shareholders and relevant stakeholders?

4.7 ☐ Enforced with minimal bureaucracy?

4.8 ☐ When appropriate, varied to take account of the law and custom of the countries of operation?

4.9 ☐ Reviewed and justified at appropriate times?

What action, if any, is required?...

B. Set strategy and structure

B.1 Review and evaluate present and future opportunities, threats and risks in the external environment; and current and future strengths, weaknesses and risks relating to the company

☐ *Does your board do such a review?*
If so, does this review...

1.1 ☐ Recognise that past trends cannot simply be extrapolated into the future?

1.2 ☐ Include imaginative and iconoclastic thinking?

1.3 ☐ Consciously seek to make balanced collective judgements, taking individual biases into account?

1.4 ☐ Incorporate input from external specialists when appropriate?

1.5 ☐ Evaluate the probable risks attached to different future outcomes?

1.6 ☐ Compare various measures of performance against those of other relevant companies and incorporate the comparisons into the review?

1.7 ☐ Take account of the wider environment, including possible legislative, regulatory, technological, economic, social and environmental changes?

What action, if any, is required?...

B.2 Determine strategic options, select those to be pursued, and decide the means to implement and support them

☐ *Does your board determine strategic options, review and select those to be pursued, and decide the resources, contingency plans and means to support them?*
If so, are the options...

2.1 ☐ Considered in an unfettered and creative way?

2.2 ☐ Evaluated systematically in relation to the company's mission and values?

2.3 ☐ Likely to support the achievement of the company's goals?

Once options are chosen, are they....

2.4 ☐ Resourced effectively, taking into account likely risks, financial considerations, and likely capabilities?

2.5 ☐ Supported by effective measures to detect potential success or failure?

2.6 ☐ Supported with realistic contingency plans in the event of failure or unexpected developments, particularly competitors' likely reactions?

2.7 ☐ 'Owned' by the board?

What action, if any, is required?...

B. Set strategy and structure

B.3 Determine the business strategies and plans that underpin the corporate strategy

☐ *Are business strategies and plans for different parts of the company...*

3.1 ☐ Regularly reviewed by the main board?

3.2 ☐ Consistent with corporate strategy, objectives and plans?

3.3 ☐ Based on knowledge of the market environment, particularly what customers are likely to want, and consistent with likely changes in the market environment?

3.4 ☐ Taking account of new entrants and potential new entrants into the marketplace and industrial sector?

3.5 ☐ Reviewed to exploit mutuality between business units?

3.6 ☐ Tested for their feasibility and full exploitation of opportunities and potential resources?

3.7 ☐ Likely to consider fully the basis for added-value innovations and changes in know-how?

3.8 ☐ Understood and vigorously supported by management?

3.9 ☐ Meeting good practice standards elsewhere and improved if necessary?

3.10 ☐ Monitored with specific action-based and dated 'milestones'?

3.11 ☐ Supported by appropriate project plans and management reports?

3.12 ☐ Consistent with legal requirements and ethical guidelines?

3.13 ☐ Taking account of associated risk and reward?

3.14 ☐ Taking into account, when appropriate, the views of shareholders and relevant stakeholders?

What action, if any, is required?...

B.4 Ensure that the company's organisational structure and capability are appropriate for implementing the chosen strategies

☐ *Does the organisational structure...*

4.1 ☐ Aid the implementation of the corporate and business strategies?

4.2 ☐ Enable all employees' skills/motivation to flourish?

4.3 ☐ Have an appropriate degree of hierarchy?

4.4 ☐ Promote effective two-way communications?

4.5 ☐ Ensure decisions are made in practice by the appropriate people?

4.6 ☐ Demonstrate flexibility in response to change?

Does the organisation's culture...

4.7 ☐ Encourage questioning of convention?

4.8 ☐ Encourage enterprise and innovation?

4.9 ☐ Respect and develop individuals and teams?

4.10 ☐ Encourage training that adds value to the business?

4.11 ☐ Encourage continuous learning at work?

Does your board...

4.12 ☐ Support and when necessary champion change?

4.13 ☐ Encourage employees to communicate widely and be well-informed?

4.14 ☐ Insist on efficient and effective business systems?

4.15 ☐ Promote short-and long-term performance related rewards such that individuals and teams are motivated to achieve desired goals?

What action, if any, is required?...

C. Delegate to management

C.1 Delegate authority to management, and monitor and evaluate the implementation of policies, strategies and business plans

☐ *Does your board clearly delegate authority to management and regularly review management's effectiveness? If so, are these reviews...*

1.1 ☐ Undertaken under clear terms of reference?

1.2 ☐ Undertaken in a manner likely to engender management commitment, support and continued integrity?

1.3 ☐ Regular, thorough and comprehensive?

1.4 ☐ Based on succinct, complete and accurate management reports?

1.5 ☐ Likely to encourage positive inputs?

1.6 ☐ Focused on causes and consequences of important variances from plan?

1.7 ☐ Focused sufficiently on management's ability and performance in anticipating, identifying and responding to change?

1.8 ☐ Likely to identify realistic and achievable corrective actions, if necessary?

1.9 ☐ Informed, when appropriate, by the views of shareholders and relevant stakeholders?

What action, if any, is required?...

C.2 Determine monitoring criteria to be used by the board

☐ *Does your board have such criteria? Do they cover the implementation of strategy, policies, plans and compliance with legal and fiduciary obligations that affect the company? If so, are they...*

2.1 ☐ Recognised as extremely important and supported as such by the entire board?

2.2 ☐ Tailored to the needs and responsibilities of individual directors and board committees?

2.3 ☐ Guided by 'best practice' standards, including those recommended by relevant professional bodies?

2.4 ☐ Established for all relevant aspects of the company's activities and the environment in which it operates, including legal and fiduciary features?

2.5 ☐ Informed by the appropriate views of shareholders and relevant stakeholders?

2.6 ☐ Formulated to cover at least profitability, cash flow, investment, risk, the protection of key assets, and the promotion of competitive advantage?

2.7 ☐ Able clearly to identify and explain trends and variances between planned and actual implementation?

2.8 ☐ Effective in providing forewarning of major risks and opportunities?

2.9 ☐ Reviewed regularly for consistency and relevance?

What action, if any, is required?...

C. Delegate to management

C.3 Ensure that internal controls are effective

☐ *Does your board ensure that internal control procedures provide reliable, valid and timely information for monitoring and controlling operations and performance? If so, are internal control procedures...*

3.1 ☐ Adequately resourced and regularly reviewed for their integrity, reliability, relevance, cost effectiveness and completeness?

3.2 ☐ Tested by internal and external audits, including non-financial parameters?

Is the information provided by the procedures...

3.3 ☐ Timely enough for directors properly to prepare themselves?

3.4 ☐ Consistent with information from the company's planning and control systems?

3.5 ☐ Informed by recent activities?

What action, if any, is required?...

C.4 Communicate with senior management

☐ *Does your board (and/or its members) do this?*
If so, does it...

4.1 ☐ Communicate clearly, quickly and honestly, and in a way that engenders constructive feedback?

4.2 ☐ Consider managers' capabilities when reviewing strategies?

4.3 ☐ Motivate and develop managers to improve their effectiveness?

4.4 ☐ Adequately acknowledge good and bad performance?

4.5 ☐ Consider managers' performance when selecting executive directors?

4.6 ☐ Consider the structure of the management team in the light of their performance?

What action, if any, is required?...

D. Exercise accountability to shareholders and be responsible to relevant stakeholders

D.1 Ensure that communications both to and from shareholders and relevant stakeholders are effective

☐ *Does your board ensure these communications are made? Are these communications based upon a policy of accessibility and openness? Is the board accountable to shareholders for company actions? Is the board appropriately responsible for relations with relevant stakeholders? If so, are these communications from the company...*

1.1 ☐ Focused upon vision, mission, values and policies led (or clearly delegated) by directors?

1.2 ☐ Relevant, consistent, accurate, and cost-effective?

1.3 ☐ Unbiased, for example with respect to special groups or minorities? .

1.4 ☐ Likely to meet shareholders' and/or stakeholders' reasonable expectations, in terms of their quantity, quality, timing and form?

1.5 ☐ Regularly reviewed, compared with best practice elsewhere, and improved if necessary?

1.6 ☐ In compliance with the needs of commercial security and any regulatory requirements, where appropriate?

1.7 ☐ Helpful in promoting the interests of the company?

If so, are these communications to the company...

1.8 ☐ Brought to the board's attention, when and where sufficiently important?

1.9 ☐ Summarised regularly?

What action, if any, is required?...

D.2 Understand and take into account the interests of shareholders and relevant stakeholders

☐ *Does your board do this?*
When doing so, does the board...

2.1 ☐ Ensure that key parties are regularly identified and reviewed?

2.2 ☐ Endeavour to understand the present and likely future interests and concerns of each of these parties?

2.3 ☐ Know the way shareholders and stakeholders can have influence over the company's present objectives, values, policies and activities and may affect future objectives, values, policies, and activities?

2.4 ☐ Seek to anticipate the impact of future possible environmental, technical, political and other developments on the stance and behaviour of shareholders and stakeholders?

2.5 ☐ Ensure compliance with legal and regulatory requirements?

2.6 ☐ Ensure compliance with the company's ethical policy, if there is one?

What action, if any, is required?...

D. Exercise accountability to shareholders and be responsible to relevant stakeholders

D.3 Monitor relations with shareholders and relevant stakeholders by the gathering and evaluation of appropriate information

Does your board monitor these relations?
If so, are the systems and methods...

3.1 ☐ Reliable?

3.2 ☐ Legal and ethical?

3.3 ☐ Capable of providing information that is both regular and timely in order to facilitate effective action?

3.4 ☐ Robust in times of crisis?

3.5 ☐ Capable of informing the board about the possible risks, costs and benefits of (mis)managing relations?

If so, is the information...

3.6 ☐ Realistic and objective?

3.7 ☐ Relevant for timely decision-making and action?

What action, if any, is required?...

D.4 Promote the goodwill and support of shareholders and relevant stakeholders

☐ *Does your board promote goodwill and support? If so,...*

4.1 ☐ Is the board collectively committed to enhancing goodwill with shareholders and relevant stakeholders?

4.2 ☐ Are responsibilities for liaising with shareholders and with different stakeholders clear?

4.3 ☐ Do procedures exist for managing routine relationships with shareholders and with relevant stakeholders?

4.4 ☐ Do established procedures exist for managing relationships at times of crisis (for example, major redundancy programmes, environmental disasters, contested take-over bids)?

4.5 ☐ If crises have not occurred, has the effectiveness of the procedures been tested?

What action, if any, is required?...

Standards
for the Board

PART FOUR:
Knowledge and Skills

Attributes and areas of competence

Research shows that boards operate in ways very different from conventional teams, especially in fashioning creative solutions out of the competing and conflicting views which different directors can bring to board discussions. Although it is essential that board members are prepared to collaborate with colleagues on the board, it is equally important that they maintain their independence and avoid the 'group think' which leads to poor collective decisions. Effective boards will have a good balance of well-chosen, competent directors, who, with the chairman's leadership, provide a cohesive working group to shape the destiny of the company, safeguard its interests and ensure its profitable performance.

Achieving that balance and choosing the right directors is not easy. However this section of the *Standards* can be helpful when preparing to make those decisions. It identifies a number of personal attributes – abilities, skills, motivations and values – and some key areas of knowledge exhibited by company directors.

By using the checklists to identify which characteristics are relevant to the circumstances and needs of a particular board and which are possessed by the existing directors, gaps which need to be filled can be identified. This may help in specifying what to look for when recruiting a new director and the areas where existing directors could be developed. The criteria for assessing an individual's specific personal attributes must be clearly established in relation to the board's particular requirements.

The personal attributes – each of which is briefly described – can be classified into six groups relating to specific aspects of company direction. They are relevant to a director's role, whether as chairman, managing director, executive or non-executive director.

These groups are:

- *Strategic perception*
- *Decision-making*
- *Analysis and the use of information*
- *Communication*
- *Interaction with others*
- *Achievement of results*

Many of these attributes are components of **leadership**, by which is meant the ability to conduct the company's affairs and to govern, guide and motivate others. The board of directors leads the company and whether it does this well or badly depends in part upon the personal attributes of its members. Of course, it is unlikely that any one individual will have all the personal attributes listed, but each of those deemed necessary for a particular board should be possessed by at least one director. Ideally, there should be a good balance of individuals, whose strengths and weaknesses are complementary.

Personalities are important too. For example, boards composed entirely of thrusting, action-orientated people are unlikely to spend sufficient time addressing issues which will affect the company's long-term future. Someone must be reflective and provide the original thinking and ideas.

Each board will have to choose its membership in its own way but should take characteristics like these into account in order to build an effective working group.

Ultimately directors need to know – or know how to find out – everything that is relevant to their responsibilities. Ignorance is no excuse. However each company and each board is unique; it is therefore impossible to produce a comprehensive and definitive list of all the elements of knowledge and understanding which a director should possess.

However, some key areas of directors' knowledge and understanding are provided on pages 72-78. The list is illustrative rather than comprehensive, covering the main areas expected to be found around a board table, although the breadth and depth of these requirements will vary according to the circumstances and demands faced by a particular board.

The areas of knowledge required by directors are always changing. In preparing the list, not all function-specific and specialist knowledge (which may or may not be sought from outside the board) has been included. Neither have the areas of knowledge and understanding required principally of a management role rather than that of a director been included – these are addressed by the *Senior Management Standards: Second Edition* (1998) produced by the Management Charter Initiative.

STRATEGIC PERCEPTION

Change-orientation

Alert and responsive to the need for change. Encourages new initiatives and the implementation of new policies, structures and practices.

Creativity

Generates and recognises imaginative solutions and innovations.

Foresight

Is able to imagine possible future states and characteristics of the company in a future environment.

Organisational awareness

Is aware of the company's strengths and weaknesses and of the likely impact of the board's decisions upon them.

Perspective

Rises above the immediate problem or situation and sees the wider issues and implications. Is able to relate disparate facts and see all relevant relationships.

Strategic awareness

Is aware of the various factors which determine the company's opportunities and threats (for example, shareholder, stakeholder, market, technological, environmental and regulatory factors).

DECISION-MAKING

Critical faculty

Probes the facts, challenges assumptions, identifies the (dis)advantages of proposals, provides counter arguments, ensures discussions are penetrating.

Decisiveness

Shows a readiness to take decisions and take action. Is able to make up his/her mind.

Judgement

Makes sensible decisions or recommendations by weighing evidence, considers reasonable assumptions, the ethical dimension, and factual information.

ANALYSIS AND THE USE OF INFORMATION

Consciousness of detail

Insists that sufficiently detailed and reliable information is taken account of, and reported as necessary.

Eclecticism

Systematically seeks all possible relevant information from a variety of sources.

Numeracy

Assimilates numerical and statistical information accurately, understands its derivation and makes sensible, sound interpretations.

Problem recognition

Identifies problems and identifies possible or actual causes.

COMMUNICATION

Listening skills

Listens dispassionately, intently and carefully so that key points are recalled and taken into account, questioning when necessary to ensure understanding.

Openness

Is frank and open when communicating. Willing to admit errors and shortcomings.

Verbal fluency

Speaks clearly, audibly and has good diction. Concise, avoids jargon and tailors content to the audience's needs.

Presentation skills

Conveys ideas, images and words in a way which shows empathy with the audience.

Written communication skills

Written matter is readily intelligible; ideas, information and opinions are conveyed accurately, clearly and concisely.

Responsiveness

Is able to invite and accept feedback.

INTERACTION WITH OTHERS

Confidence

Is aware of own strengths and weaknesses. Is assured when dealing with others. Able to take charge of a situation when appropriate.

Co-ordination skills

Adopts appropriate interpersonal styles and methods in guiding the board towards task accomplishment. Fosters co-operation and effective teamwork.

Flexibility

Adopts a flexible (but not compliant) style when interacting with others. Takes their views into account and changes position when appropriate.

Presence

Makes a strong positive impression on first meeting. Has authority and credibility, establishes rapport quickly.

Integrity

Is truthful and trustworthy and can be relied upon to keep his/her word. Does not have double standards and does not compromise on ethical and legal matters.

Learning ability

Seeks and acquires new knowledge and skills from multiple sources, including board experience.

Motivation

Inspires others to achieve goals by ensuring a clear understanding of what needs to be achieved and by showing commitment, enthusiasm, encouragement and support.

Persuasiveness

Persuades others to give their agreement and commitment; in face of conflict, uses personal influence to achieve consensus and/or agreement.

Sensitivity

Shows an understanding of the feelings and needs of others, and a willingness to provide personal support or to take other actions as appropriate.

ACHIEVEMENT OF RESULTS

Business acumen

Has the ability to identify opportunities to increase the company's business advantage.

Delegation skills

Distinguishes between what should be done by others or by himself/herself. Allocates decision-making or other tasks to appropriate colleagues and subordinates.

Exemplar

Sets challenging but achievable goals and standards of performance for self and others.

Drive

Shows energy, vitality and commitment.

Resilience

Maintains composure and effectiveness in the face of adversity, setbacks, opposition or unfairness.

Risk acceptance

Is prepared to take action that involves calculated risk in order to achieve a desired benefit or advantage.

Tenacity

Stays with a position or plan of action until the desired objectives are achieved or require adaptation.

Some key areas of applied knowledge

The following is the result largely of experience with the IoD Company Direction Programme, which has been taught for many years at a number of business schools in the UK and at the IoD, and is now available in distance-learning format. Several thousand company directors have taken this Programme. Many focus groups of company directors and academics have contributed to defining a minimum set of knowledge and techniques required by a company director in the practice of his/her profession in a variety of different contexts, which constitutes the basis of the Programme.

The areas of knowledge it is recommended that company directors are cognisant of are:

- *The role of company director and the board*
- *Strategic business direction*
- *Basic principles and practice of finance and accounting*
- *Effective marketing strategy*
- *Human resource direction*
- *Improving business performance*
- *Organising for tomorrow*

The cognitive skills required by good practice with respect to the identified subject areas include:

knowledge: *the ability to recognise and recall a piece of information;*

understanding: *the ability to make use of information in a specific way depending on the situation;*

application: *the ability to select an appropriate known principle in a new situation, to restructure data in a suitable form, and to apply the principle;*

analysis: *the ability to split a concept, event or situation into its constituent parts.*

In what follows, the terms "knowledge" and "know" are sometimes used to summarise all four of these cognitive skills. In general, the higher the order of cognitive skill possessed in reference to a subject area, the better.

The requisite areas of knowledge – understanding – application – analysis are:

The role of company director and the board

A director should be aware of his or her role and appreciate the crucial differences between management and direction. Directors should have an understanding of the legal framework within which they operate. A director should have a good understanding of a board's operation and how to ensure its effectiveness.

In particular, do you and your fellow directors know, understand, apply and analyse (as appropriate)...

☐ the legal status of a company and the purpose of the Memorandum and Articles of Association?

☐ the differences between ownership, direction and management?

☐ the role, purpose and principal tasks of a board of directors?

☐ the complexity of the board's task and the dilemmas with which boards are frequently confronted?

☐ good practice in organising and running a board, including the effective use of appropriate board committees?

☐ the criteria which may be used to assess board performance?

☐ what is board leadership, including defining and communicating the corporate mission, vision and values?

☐ the factors affecting the composition, structure and style of the board?

☐ the roles of different directors, particularly executive and non-executive directors, managing director and chairman, and the roles of company secretary and advisers to the board?

☐ the major laws and regulations with which companies and directors in the UK must comply and the legal duties and potential liabilities of individual directors and the board, including those arising from work as a member of a board committee?

☐ directors' fiduciary duties and the duties of skill, care and diligence?

☐ both national and European laws and regulations relating to trade descriptions, consumer protection, contracts, sale of goods, the environment, mis-representation, intellectual property, design protection, inventions, confidential information and many other activities sufficiently to be able to seek professional advice if needed?

Strategic business direction

Being charged with determining the company's strategic direction, a director should know and understand the issues and processes involved in formulating, implementing and controlling the company's corporate and business strategies.

In particular, do you and your fellow directors know, understand, apply and analyse (as appropriate)...

☐ the determination of vision, mission and values?

☐ what strategy is and why it is important?

☐ how to identify the board's main strategic tasks?

☐ the role of the board in strategy formulation, analysis and implementation, and its distinction from that of management?

☐ how to determine organisational structures according to strategy?

- [ ] how to assess strategic concepts, particularly core competencies, cost leadership and differentiation, in relation to your own organisation?

- [ ] different ways of analysing alternative strategies, of getting strategic plans implemented, and the critical factors making for successful implementation?

- [ ] how to build capabilities via mergers and acquisitions/disposals?

- [ ] how to link the strategic goals of a company to the day-to-day activities of the firm, taking into account organisational resistance to change?

Basic principles and practice of finance and accounting

A director should have a sound background knowledge of company accounting, financial language and concepts, and relevant financial tools and techniques.

In particular, do you and your fellow directors know, understand, apply and analyse (as appropriate)...

- [ ] the role of the company auditor and the audit committee?

- [ ] simple financial analysis to evaluate and monitor the state of a company?

- [ ] what are the various sources of finance available to a company and what are their relative advantages and disadvantages?

- [ ] how to match financial resources to company strategy and allocate financial resources to different areas?

- [ ] financial language and concepts?

- [ ] the elements within a financial planning process?

- [ ] the level of detail and the frequency of reporting that directors need to direct their business effectively?

☐ the profit and loss statement, the balance sheet, and cashflow statement?

☐ the difference between the management accounts used in the direction of a business and the statutory financial reports of a company?

☐ the time-value of money and the common techniques of project appraisal?

Effective marketing strategy

A director should have an appreciation of the vital role of successful marketing strategies and an understanding of how to create, implement and control these strategies so as to create customer value and to improve a company's market performance.

In particular, do you and your fellow directors know, understand, apply and analyse (as appropriate)…

☐ the key concepts of marketing and their importance in business?

☐ the changes in your market place, using a marketing audit checklist?

☐ the major techniques and tools of marketing analysis?

☐ how to define markets in terms of customers, products, competitors and distributors?

☐ the principles of customer purchasing behaviour?

☐ actual and potential sources of competitive advantage?

☐ how to analyse and formulate alternative marketing strategies?

☐ that corporate strategies succeed or fail to the extent that they create customer value, and that net present value can be created only by superior market performance?

Human resource direction

A director should be aware of the importance of employing the right people with the right skills, and encouraging their commitment, involvement and contribution.

In particular, do you and your fellow directors know, understand, apply and analyse (as appropriate)...

☐ appropriate human resource policies in the light of overall corporate strategy?

☐ relevant recruitment and induction policies to support the overall business strategy?

☐ training and development policy?

☐ rewards, motivation and commitment, particularly in the context of change?

☐ communications within the organisation, both formal and informal?

☐ the fundamentals of employment law?

Improving business performance

A director should understand the link between total quality techniques and business results and what are the determining factors in improving the business's performance.

In particular, do you and your fellow directors know, understand, apply and analyse (as appropriate)...

☐ the strategic implications of customer satisfaction, quality, perceived value, cost and market positioning?

☐ how the concepts of quality management may enhance the achievement of corporate goals?

☐ how added value is created in the business?

☐ the value chain in the business?

☐ the key business processes, in order to identify where improvements can be made?

☐ the bases of competitive advantage for the company and how these may change?

☐ the expertise, motivation, organisation, skills, knowledge and supportive investment of the company's employees?

☐ the likely implications of the rapid developments in IT and communications technology on the company's operations?

☐ the assessment of risks and threats to the company and the adequacy of contingency plans?

Organising for tomorrow

Charged with ensuring the company's capabilities meet the demands of the corporate strategy, a director should know how modern companies respond to a changing environment.

In particular, do you and your fellow directors know, understand, apply and analyse (as appropriate)...

☐ what is involved in corporate vision, values, mission and culture?

☐ how to match organisational structures and capabilities according to strategy, culture and corporate values?

☐ how to map the different forces for change in an organisation?

☐ how to lead change through the appropriate type of leadership?

☐ the board's role in organisational development and the personal development process?

Standards
for the Board

APPENDIX:
Summary of the Combined Code
on Corporate Governance

Introduction

- The remit of the *Committee on Corporate Governance* (Hampel Committee, 1998) was to review and consolidate the earlier work of the *Committee on the Financial Aspects of Corporate Governance* (Cadbury Committee, 1992) and the work of *Directors' Remuneration: Report of a Study Group* (Greenbury Committee, 1995) and develop clear guidelines on corporate governance standards. In addition to issuing a *Final Report*, it also drafted the *Combined Code* on corporate governance. The major elements of the Combined Code are summarised here.

- The London Stock Exchange's Listing Rules have since been amended to require listed companies to provide a statement of compliance with the Code and a detailed directors' remuneration report for accounting periods ending on or after 31 December 1998. Any areas of non-compliance must be disclosed in the Annual Report and Accounts and explained fully in the compliance statement.

- In general terms, the Code is designed to:

  - *encourage shareholders, non-executive directors and auditors to accept their legal responsibilities and scrutinise the stewardship of companies; and*

  - *impose adequate checks and balances on executive directors without restricting unduly the exercise of enterprise by boards of directors.*

Boards of directors

Every listed company should be headed by an effective board of directors which governs the company. The Code provides that:

THE BOARD

- The board should meet regularly.

- The board should have a formal schedule of matters specifically reserved to it for decision.

- The board should have timely information in a form and of appropriate quality to enable the board to discharge its duties effectively.

- The board should have a formal, transparent procedure for the appointment of new directors; and, unless the board is small, a nomination committee should be established to make recommendations to the board on all new board appointments. A majority of the members of this committee should be non-executive directors and the chairman should be either the chairman of the board or a non-executive director. The chairman and members of the nomination committee should be identified in the Annual Report.

- An individual should receive appropriate training on the first occasion that he or she is appointed to the board of a listed company, and subsequently as necessary.

- The board should have a requirement that all directors submit themselves for re-election at least every three years. Non-executive directors should be appointed for specified terms and reappointment should not be automatic. All directors should be subject to election by shareholders at the first opportunity after their appointment, and to re-election thereafter at intervals of no more than three years. Biographical details of directors submitted for election or re-election should be provided to shareholders.

THE COMPANY SECRETARY

- The Code supports the Cadbury view that the company secretary should play an important role in providing advice to directors. All directors should have access to the advice and services of the company secretary.

- The company secretary should also be responsible to the board for ensuring that board procedures are followed and that applicable rules and regulations are complied with.

- Any question of the removal of the company secretary should be a matter for the board as a whole.

BOARD COMMITTEES

- Listed companies are required to maintain separate independent committees dealing with audit, remuneration, and nomination, each of which should have written terms of reference.

THE CHAIRMAN

- There should be a clearly accepted division of responsibilities at the head of the company between the chairman and the managing director. The justification is to try and ensure a balance of power and authority, such that no one individual has unfettered powers of decision. A decision to combine the posts of chairman and managing director in one person should be publicly explained.

- The chairman has an obligation to disseminate information properly and ensure that all directors are adequately briefed on issues arising at board meetings.

BOARD COMPOSITION

- Both Cadbury and Hampel stress that the board should include independent non-executive directors of sufficient calibre and number for their views to carry significant weight in the board's decisions. "Independent" directors are defined as persons who "apart from directors' fees and shareholdings [are] independent of the management and free from any business or other relationships which could materially interfere with the exercise of the independent judgement" (*Committee on the Financial Aspects of Corporate Governance*, 1992). The majority of non-executive directors should be independent. Non-executive directors considered by the board to be independent should be identified in the Annual Report.

- The balance of executive and non-executive directors should be such that no individual or small group of individuals can dominate the board's decision-taking. Non-executive directors should comprise not less than one-third of the board.

Remuneration

- Levels of remuneration should be sufficient to attract and retain the executive directors needed to run the company successfully. The component parts of executive directors' remuneration should be structured so as to link rewards with corporate and individual performance. Recommendations on the design of performance-based remuneration are included as a schedule to the Combined Code.

- Companies should establish a formal and transparent procedure for developing policy on executive remuneration and for fixing the remuneration packages of individual directors. No director should be involved in determining his or her own remuneration.

- The company's annual report should contain a statement of remuneration policy and details of the remuneration of each director

Relations with shareholders

- According to Cadbury, "the shareholders' role in governance is to appoint the directors and auditors and satisfy themselves that an appropriate governance structure is in place". To meet their obligations, shareholders must participate actively in the affairs of the company and make considered use of their votes. In order to do this effectively, they must be fully informed. The Hampel Report emphasises that the overriding objective of listed companies is "the preservation and… enhancement over time of their shareholders' investment".

- The Code states two key principles:

  - *Companies should be ready, where practicable, to enter into dialogue with institutional shareholders based on a mutual understanding of objectives. Section 2 of the Code contains recommendations on improving the dialogue between listed companies and institutional investors, as well as encouraging institutional investors to make considered use of their votes.*

  - *Boards should use the Annual General Meeting to communicate with private investors and encourage their participation.*

- The Code also requires, *inter alia*, an end to the practice of bundling resolutions, such that shareholders have to reject sound proposals in order to vote down one unacceptable element. Distinct issues require separate resolutions.

- At least 20 working days notice of the AGM (the Act specifies 21 days) must be given, and the chairmen of each of the three key governance committees (audit, remuneration and nomination) should be present to answer questions.

Accountability and audit

The Code makes recommendations in three main areas of accountability:

Financial reporting

The board should present a balanced and understandable assessment of the company's position and prospects by ensuring that:

- *both directors and auditors explain their reporting responsibilities in financial reports;*
- *interim and other price sensitive reports are balanced and understandable; and*
- *financial reports are on a "going-concern" basis, including an explanation of assumptions and qualifications.*

Internal Control

The board should maintain a sound system of internal controls to safeguard the shareholders' investment and the company's assets by:

- *conducting an annual review of such controls and reporting to shareholders;*
- *reviewing the need for an internal audit function on a regular basis, where the company does not have one.*

Relationship with the Auditors

- The Hampel Report follows its predecessors in viewing external checks on the consistency and reliability of financial statements as a key to investor confidence. The task of the auditor is seen as being to report to shareholders on whether the company's annual accounts are properly prepared and give a true and fair view, and to review the directors' 'going concern' statement, the extent of Code compliance, and the remuneration committee's report.

- The board should establish formal and transparent arrangements for considering how the financial reporting and control principles should be applied and for maintaining an appropriate relationship with the company's auditors. The Code recommends that:

  - *the audit committee should review the scope, results and effectiveness of the audit and ensure that, where the auditor also provides non-audit services, this is carefully reviewed;*

  - *the independence of the audit committee is enhanced by its having at least three non-executive director members, a majority of whom should be independent and identified in the Annual Report.*

Books for Directors from the IoD

The IoD publishes a number of authoritative business publications written specifically for practising and aspiring directors.

Standards for the Board is part of the Good Practice for Directors Series. The series also includes the best-selling business publication *Guidelines for Directors.*

GUIDELINES FOR DIRECTORS

Do you know:

- *How a director's duties are defined by law?*
- *What is the purpose of the Articles and Memorandum of Association?*
- *What information a company must disclose?*
- *What is the role of the chairman?*
- *How to evaluate board performance?*
- *Who the law can treat as a director?*

Guidelines for Directors offers a practical guide to the role, duties and responsibilities of directors.

For more details on IoD Publications contact:

Product Marketing Department
Institute of Directors
116 Pall Mall
London SWIY 5ED
Tel 0171 766 8766
Fax 0171 766 8787

IoD Director Development

The Institute of Directors is the UK's leading authority on senior manager and director-level training and development. It focuses on raising the professional standards of business leaders through the provision of an unequalled range of development products and services that include:

- *Open Courses*
- *Director Programmes*
- *Flexible Learning*
- *In-company Training*
- *Board Consultancy*
- *Individual Executive Coaching*

From a one-off course to a complex programme of board development, the Institute of Directors continues to meet the changing professional needs of all senior executives, whatever their experience, company size or type of business.

For further information please contact:

Director Development
Institute of Directors
116 Pall Mall
London SW1Y 5ED
Tel: 0171 766 8800
Fax: 0171 766 8765
Email: cdd@iod.co.uk
Web: www.iod.co.uk

Membership
of the IoD

Discover the benefits of IoD Membership.

- *Free business information and advice from experts*

- *Meeting and entertainment facilities in prestigious surroundings in central London, Leeds, Nottingham and Edinburgh*

- *Opportunities to meet regularly with fellow directors from all industries*

- *A business travel service offering competitive rates and significant discounts at Hilton Hotels worldwide*

- *Free access to 16 executive airport lounges in the UK*

- *Leading-edge professional development tailored to your needs, including courses, conferences and publications*

- *Preferential rates on insurance against your liabilities as a director*

- *An exclusive package of products and services including a Visa Gold Card with no annual fee*, preferential rates on personal loans* and many more*

*Subject to status and available only to UK residents.

If you are a director, partner, sole proprietor or company secretary and would like more information about membership of the Institute of Directors, please contact:

Membership Development Department
Institute of Directors
116 Pall Mall
London SW1Y 5ED
Tel: 0171 766 8888.

IoD Professional Development

The IoD works with directors, policy makers, academics, and the media to raise boardroom standards across the UK. We focus on defining and promoting professional standards for directors, and helping them attain high levels of expertise and effectiveness by improving their knowledge and skills.

In promoting new thinking and practice concerning corporate governance, boardroom practice, director professionalism, company law reform and related issues, we also aim to promote the idea that "Business Matters" to all parts of society in order to encourage outstanding talent to work in business, and to provide a sympathetic background in which business can flourish.

In addition to helping company directors, our work has also involved helping elements of the public sector improve their governance:

- *In 1995, the IoD was invited by the NHS Executive to develop* **Criteria for NHS Boards**, *published in 1996.*

- *In 1996, the IoD was invited by the Lord Chancellor's Department to develop* **Standards for Magistrates' Courts Committees**, *published in 1996.*

- *In 1997, the IoD was invited by the Department of Trade and Industry to develop* **A Development Guide for Business Link Board Members** *and* **Board Development for Business Links**, *both published in 1998.*

We also set and administer the IoD's professional standards, including the profession of Chartered Director and the prestigious Diploma in Company Direction.

For further information please contact:

Professional Development Department
Institute of Directors
116 Pall Mall, London SW1Y 5ED
Tel: 0171 451 3106. Fax: 0171 839 9264
Email: profdev@iod.co.uk